The Step-by-Step Way to Draw Ninja

A Fun and Easy Drawing Book to Learn How to Draw Ninjas

By

Kristen Diaz

License Notes

All rights to the this Book are the sole property of the Author and no part of this Book, whether in part or whole, shall be copied, distributed, scanned, posted, shared or sold without express permission by the Author.

The content of the Book is meant for the Reader's entertainment and information. The Author accepts no liability in the case of damages, commercially or personally, incurred in the execution of information. The reader accepts all personal risk when following the guidelines, directions, opinions and instructions in the content

Table of Contents

Introduction

Becoming a great artist requires creativity, patience and practice. These habits can flourish in children when they start to develop them at a young age. We believe our guide will teach your child the discipline and patience required to not just learn to draw well, but to use those qualities in everything they do. Your job as a parent is to work with your child and encourage them when stuck and feel like giving up.

The world of art is an amazing way for you and your child to communicate and bond. When you open this book and start to create with your little one, you will delight in the things you learn about them and they will feel closer to you. Your support and gentle suggestions will help them be more patient with themselves and soon they will take the time needed to create spectacular drawings of which you can both be proud.

This guide is useful for parents as it teaches fundamentals of drawing and simple techniques. By following this book with your child, adults will learn patience and develop their skills as a child's most important teacher. By spending a few hours together you will develop a strong connection and learn the best ways of communicating with each other. It is truly a rewarding experience when you and your child create a masterpiece by working together!

How to Draw Cartoon Ninja Attacking

STEP 1

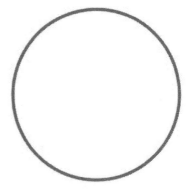

Draw a circle on the right upper part of the paper for the base of the head.

STEP 2

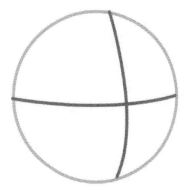

Divide the circle into sections with a curve vertical and horizontal line.

STEP 3

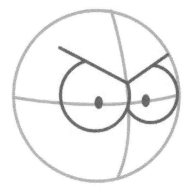

Draw an angled line shape like letter "V" along the upper part of the circle for the outline of the eyebrows. Draw the outline of the eyes with semi-circles below the eyebrows with a tiny oval inside each for the pupils.

STEP 4

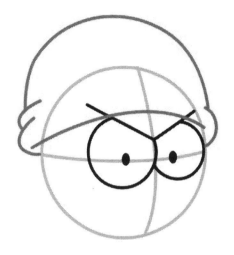

Draw the outline of the scarf enclosing the top part of his head that looks like an inverted bowl.

STEP 5

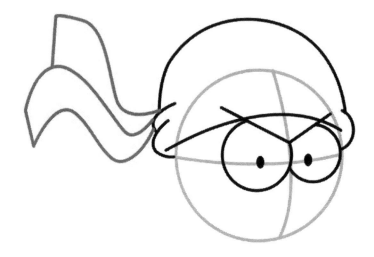

Draw the outline of the end part of the scarf with curve lines

from the left side of the scarf going to the left side of the paper.

STEP 6

Trace the outline of both sides of the head going down for the base of the neck. Draw a horizontal curve line from the left side of the eye going to the right for the outline of the mask.

STEP 7

Draw the base of the neck with diagonal lines from the bottom of the head going down with a circle at the end for the base of the body.

STEP 8

Draw the base of the right arm going horizontally to the right with the base of the hand at the end showing four fingers. Draw a small circle for the elbow.

STEP 9

Draw the base of the left arm going diagonally up to the left with a small circle and the base of the hand at the end clenched into fist.

STEP 10

Draw the base of the katana with the handle passing through the left hand. The katana is pointing diagonally down to the left.

Draw the base of the right leg with curve lines from the lower right bottom part of the circle going diagonally down with a small circle for the knee and the base of the shoe at the end pointing towards the right.

STEP 12

Draw the base of the left leg along the left bottom part of the circle going diagonally down to the left with a small circle for the knee and the base of the shoe along the righty lower part. The left leg appears to be bended towards the back.

STEP 13

Draw the outline of the collar around the neck then trace the outline of the right arm and hand.

STEP 14

Trace the outline of the left arm, hand and katana. Draw the
details of the katana as shown.

STEP 15

Trace the outline both sides of the body then draw parallel curve

line that forms a band along the middle part of the circle.

STEP 16

Trace the outline of the left leg and shoe. draw a small vertical curve line along the bottom part of the shoe.

STEP 17

Trace the outline of the right leg and shoe. draw the details of the

shoe with curve lines.

STEP 18

Final outline. Erase all unnecessary base lines.

STEP 19

You have to color it! Grey for the scarf, mask, suit, gloves and shoes. Light brown for the face. White and black for the eyes. Dark grey for the collar, lower arm, waist band and lower leg. Grey, light grey, yellow and brown for the katana. That's it! Cartoon Ninja Attacking.

How to Draw Cartoon Ninja Showing Weapon

STEP 1

Draw a circle along the middle upper part of the paper for the base of the head.

STEP 2

Divide the circle into sections with a diagonal line and a curve horizontal line. Draw the base of the lower part of the head with curve line shape like letter "U" enclosing the bottom part of the circle.

STEP 3

Draw the outline of the eyes shape like diagonal semi-circles
along the horizontal line dividing the circle.

STEP 4

Draw the outline of the scarf around the upper part of his head shape like an inverted bowl. Draw the outline of hair strands with angled curve lines above the eyes.

STEP 5

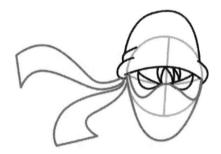

Trace the outline of the lower half of the head. Draw a curve line shape like an inverted small cursive letter "m" below the eyes for the outline of the mask. Draw the outline of both ends of the scarf with curve lines from the left side of the head going to the left part of the paper.

STEP 6

Draw the base of the neck with vertical curve lines along the
bottom part of the head with the base of the upper body at the
end.

STEP 7

Draw the base of the waist with curve lines from the bottom part of the base of the upper body going down with the base of the bikini at the end.

STEP 8

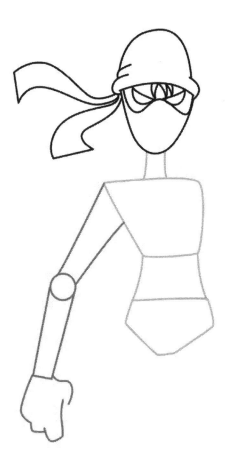

Draw the outline of the left upper arm with parallel diagonal line going down and a small circle at the end for the elbow. Draw the base of the left lower arm with parallel line from the elbow going down and the base of the and at the end clenched into fist.

STEP 9

Draw the outline of the katana pointing diagonally down to the
right and the handle passing through the left hand.

STEP 10

Draw the base of the right upper arm with parallel diagonal line going down to the right and a small circle at the end for the elbow. Draw the base of the right lower arm with short parallel diagonal line from the elbow going up to the right and the base of the hand at the end holding a weapon shape like a star as shown above.

STEP 11

Draw the base of the left leg with parallel diagonal line from the left side of the bikini going down to the left passing behind the katana and the base of the shoe at the end facing sideward to the left.

STEP 12

Draw the base of the right leg with parallel diagonal line from the right side of the bikini going down to the right and partly hidden behind the katana. Draw the base of the shoe at the end facing sideward to the right.

STEP 13

Trace the outline of the neck then draw the outline of the shirt by following the base. Draw crisscross lines along the length of the neck. Draw parallel curve line along the upper part of the sleeve.

Trace the outline of the left arm, hand and katana. Draw crisscross lines along the upper arm. Draw a curve line shape like letter "U" along the back part of the hand in line with the lower arm. Draw the details of the katana as shown above.

STEP 15

Trace the outline of the right arm, hand and weapon. Draw crisscross lines along the upper arm. Draw the outline of five fingers. Draw a small circle along the center part of the weapon.

STEP 16

Trace the outline of the left leg and shoe. Draw parallel curve vertical line along the lower leg. Draw parallel short horizontal curve line along the upper part of the shoe then draw a small curve line along the front part of the shoe. Draw the outline of the waist band with parallel diagonal curve line.

STEP 17

Trace the outline of the right leg and shoe. Draw parallel curve line along the lower leg and upper part of the shoe. Draw a small curve line along the front part of the shoe.

STEP 18

Final outline. Erase all unnecessary base lines.

STEP 19

You have to color it! Grey for the suit and lower arms. Black for the hair strands. Light brown for the face. White for the eyes. Light yellow for the neck and upper arms. Dark grey for the scarf, mask, collar, waist band, lower legs and shoes. Light grey for the weapon. Gold for the details of the sleeve and lower legs. Grey, leght grey, dark grey and yellow for the katana. That's it! Cartoon Ninja Showing Weapon.

How to Draw Cartoon Ninja with Kusarigama Weapon

STEP 1

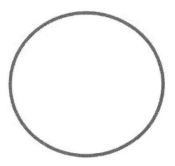

Draw a circle along the upper part of the paper for the base of the head.

STEP 2

Divide the circle into sections with a horizontal line and a curve vertical line. Draw the lower part of the head with a curve line that looks like a semi-circle enclosing the lower half of the circle.

STEP 3

Draw the outline of the eyes with vertical ovals overlapping the horizontal line dividing the head with a small oval inside each for the pupils. Draw small curve lines along the upper outer part of each eye for the eyelashes. Draw a small curve line above each eye for the eyebrows.

STEP 4

Trace the outline of the lower part of the head. Draw a curve line from the left side of the head overlapping the lower part of the eyes going to the right then curving upward.

STEP 5

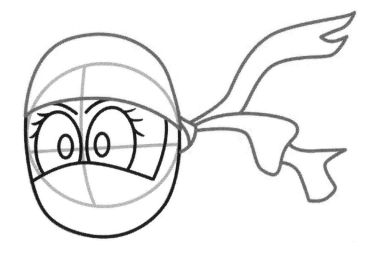

Draw the outline of the scarf along the upper part of the head shape like an inverted bowl overlapping part of the eyebrows. Draw both ends of the scarf with curve lines from the right side of the head going to the right side of the paper as shown above.

STEP 6

Draw the base of the neck with diagonal parallel line below the bottom part of the head going down with a circle at the end for the base of the body.

STEP 7

Draw the base of the left arm with parallel slim diagonal line from the left lower side of the head going up to the left with the base of the hand at the end shape like a glove.

Draw the base of the right arm with parallel slim diagonal line from the right bottom part of the head going down to the left and the base of the hand at the end shape like a pear.

Draw the outline of the kusarigama weapon with each end gripped by each hand as shown above. Draw the outline of the chain connecting both ends of the kusarigama weapon.

Draw the base of the right leg with parallel diagonal line from the right bottom part of the base of the body going down to the right with a small circle for the knee. Draw the base of the shoe at the end shape like an irregular oval pointing diagonally down to the left.

STEP 11

Draw the base of the left leg with parallel slightly curve diagonal line and the base of the shoe at the end facing sideward to the left.

Trace the outline of the right arm and hand. Draw a horizontal line dividing the length of the arm then a curve line shape like letter "U" along the back of the hand. Draw parallel vertical curve line for the fingers.

Trace the outline of the left arm and hand. Draw a small diagonal line dividing the length of the arm. Draw curve lines along the hand for the fingers.

STEP 14

Trace the outline of the kusarigama weapon then draw a curve

line parallel with the outline of the blade.

STEP 15

Trace the outline of the upper body then draw a band along the

waist. Draw the detail of the suit with parallel line shape like

letter "Y".

STEP 16

Trace the outline of the right leg and shoe. Draw a small curve line along the knee dividing the length of the leg. Draw the details of the shoe.

STEP 17

Trace the outline of the left leg and shoe. Draw the details of the shoe. Draw a small curve line along the knee.

Final outline. Erase all unnecessary base lines.

STEP 19

You have to color it! Desaturated dark blue for the scarf, mask and suit. Light brown for the face and hand. White and black for the eyes. Dark grey for the lower arms, waist band, lower legs and shoes. Light grey for the kusarigama's handle. Grey and light grey for the blade. Yellow for the chain. That's it! Cartoon Ninja With Kusarigama Weapon.

How to Draw Cartoon Ninja with Sai Weapon

STEP 1

Draw a circle along the left top part of the paper for the base of the head.

STEP 2

Divide the circle into sections with a curve vertical and horizontal line. Draw the base of the lower part of the head with curve lines from both sides of the circle going down.

STEP 3

Draw the opening of the mask with an irregular horizontal oval along the horizontal line dividing the head. Draw the outline of the eyes inside shape like a semi-circle with parallel diagonal lines on top for the eyebrows. Draw a diagonal dot inside each eye for the pupils.

STEP 4

Draw the detail of the mask with a curve end horizontal rectangle along the forehead. Draw tiny circles on each corner.

STEP 5

Draw the outline of the head enclosed in a mask by following the base. Draw the outline of both ends of the mask tied along the right side of the head and flowing towards the right.

STEP 6

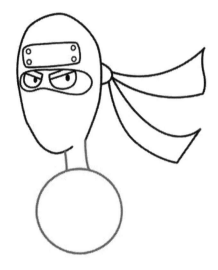

Draw the base of the neck with parallel short curve line from the bottom part of the head going down with a circle at the end for the base of the body.

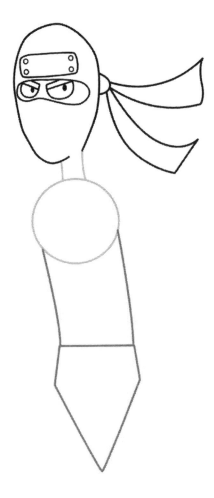

Draw parallel diagonal line from both sides of the lower part of
the circle going down to the right with the base of the bikini at
the end shape like an inverted elongated pentagon.

STEP 8

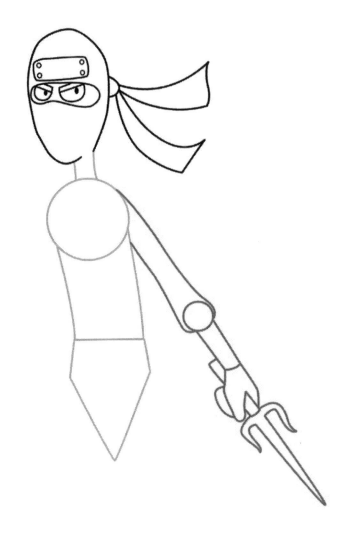

Draw the base of the right sleeve with parallel slightly curve diagonal line going down to the right and a small circle at the end for the elbow. Draw the base of the right lower arm with short parallel diagonal line from the elbow going down to the right and the base of the hand at the end. Draw the base of the sai weapon pointing diagonally down to the right with the handle passing through the hand.

Draw the base of the left sleeve with parallel slightly curve diagonal line going down to the left and a small circle at the end for the elbow. Draw the base of the lower arm from the elbow going horizontally to the left and the base of the hand at the end clenched into fist. Draw the base of the sai weapon pointing diagonally up to the right and the handle held by his hand.

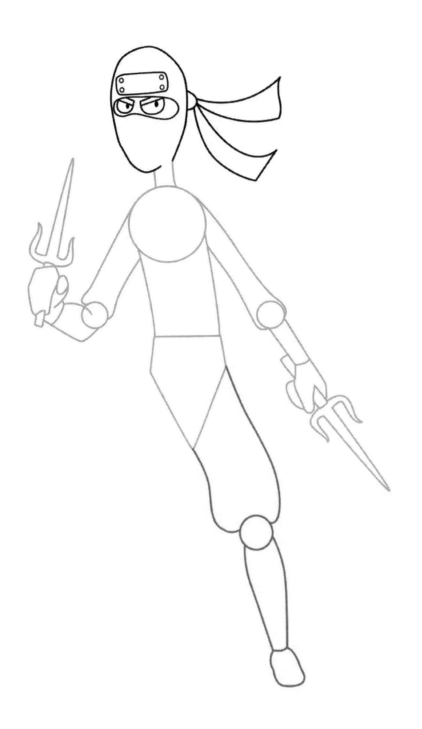

Draw the base of the right trouser with curve lines from the right side of the bikini going diagonally down to the right and a small circle at the end for the knee. Draw the base of the right lower leg with parallel curve line from the knee going diagonally down to the right and the base of the shoe at the end facing front.

STEP 11

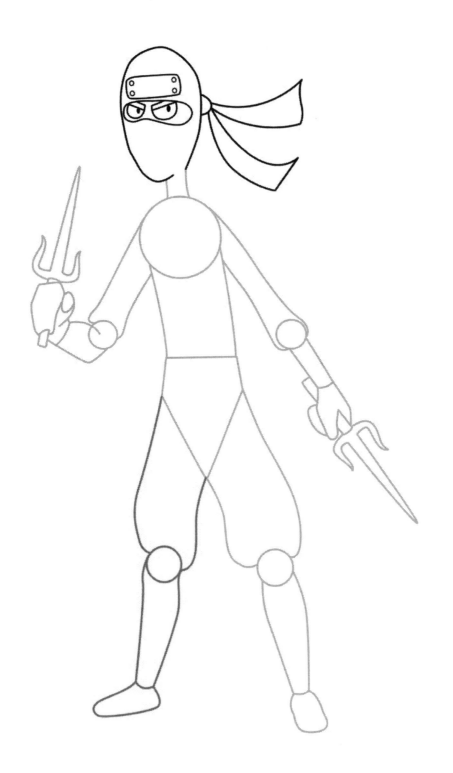

Draw the base of the left trouser with curve lines from the left side of the bikini going diagonally down to the left and a small circle at the end for the knee. Draw the base of the lower leg from the knee going diagonally down to the left and the base of the shoe at the end facing sideward to the left.

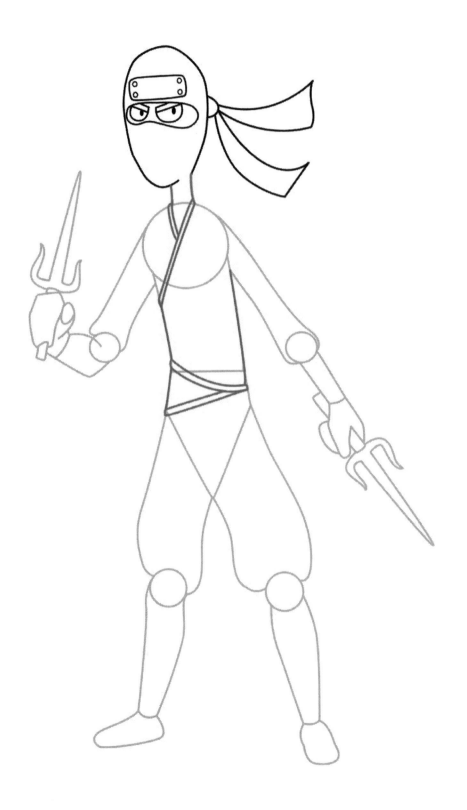

Trace the outline of the neck. Draw the outline of the collar shape like letter "Y". Trace the outline of both sides of the upper body. Draw the outline of a waist band with parallel diagonal lines forming a horizontal letter "V".

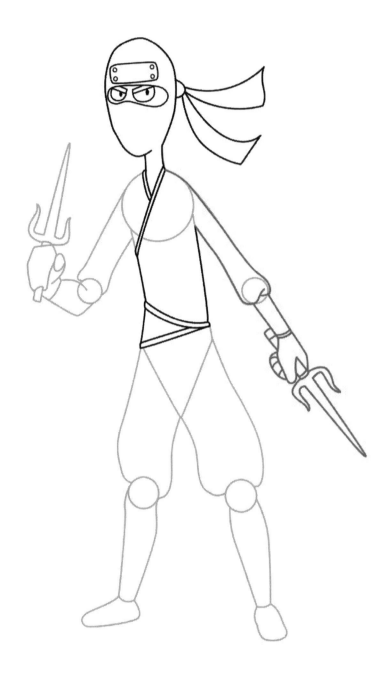

Trace the outline of the right sleeve, hand and sai weapon. Draw
the details of the weapon.

STEP 14

Trace the outline f the left sleeve, hand and weapon. Draw the
details of the hand to show the fingers.

STEP 15

Trace the outline of the right trouser and shoe. Draw the details of the shoe.

Trace the outline of the left trouser and shoe. Draw a diagonal curve line along the knee. Draw the details of the shoe.

STEP 17

Final outline. Erase all unnecessary base lines.

You have to color it! Dark grey for the mask, suit and shoes. Light grey for the details of the mask, blade of the sai weapon, collar and waist band. Light brown for the face and hands. Black for the eyebrows and pupils. White for the eyes. Desaturated red and yellow for the sai weapon's handle. Grey for the lower part of the sleeves and trousers. That's it! Cartoon Ninja With Sai Weapon.

How to Draw Chibi Running Ninja

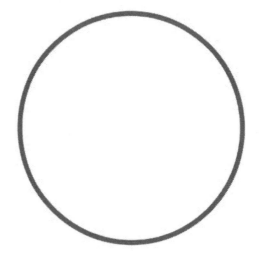

Draw a circle along the right upper part of the paper for the base

of the head.

STEP 2

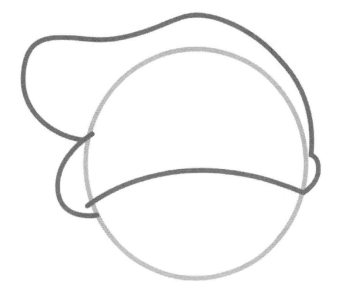

Draw the outline of the scarf enclosing the upper part of the
circle as shown above.

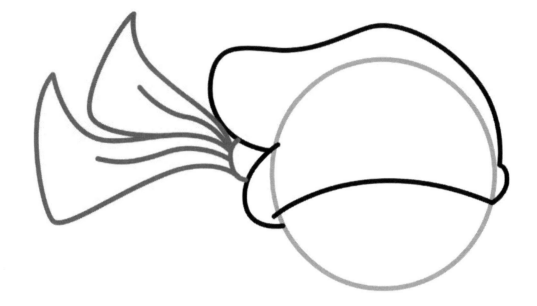

Draw the outline of both ends of the scarf tied along the left side flowing horizontally towards the left side of the paper.

Draw the outline of the mask with elongated curve line shape like horizontal inverted letter "J". Draw the outline of the left eye gong diagonally from the scarf towards the mask with a diagonal oval dot for the pupil. Draw strands of hair with angled curve lines from the right bottom part of the scarf going pointing down to the right.

Draw the base of the body from the bottom left part of the head

going diagonally down to the left and a circle at the end.

STEP 6

Draw the base of the left sleeve with parallel curve lines from the upper part of the base of the body going to the left and the base of the hand at the end.

Draw the base of the collar with curve line below the head. Draw the base of the right sleeve above the left sleeve going towards the left and the base of the hand at the end.

Trace the outline of the right side of the body then draw the
outline of the waistband with parallel curve diagonal line along
the middle part of the circle.

Draw the outline of the katana placed diagonally behind the
waist band and pointing down towards the left.

Draw the base of the left trouser from the bottom part of the
circle going diagonally down to the right and the base of the shoe
at the end facing sideward to the right.

STEP 11

Draw the base of the right trouser from the upper part of the left trouser going diagonally down to the left. Draw the base of the lower leg from the trouser going horizontally to the left with the base of the shoe at the end facing sideward and pointing down.

STEP 12

Final outline. Erase all unnecessary base lines.

STEP 13

You have to color it Dark blue for the scarf, mask and suit. Light

brown for the face and hands. White and black for the eyes.

Brown for the strands of hair. Grey for the collar, lower arms,

lower legs and shoes. Desaturated dark blue for the waist band.

Grey, light grey and yellow for the katana. That's it! Chibi

Running Ninja.

How to Draw Cute Bear Ninja

STEP 1

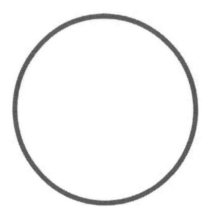

Draw a circle along the upper part of the paper for the base of the head.

STEP 2

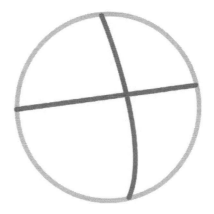

Divide the circle into sections with a diagonal line and a curve
vertical line.

STEP 3

Draw the outline of the eyes with semi-circles along the diagonal line dividing the head with a dot inside each for the pupils. Draw the outline of the nose with horizontal irregular oval overlapping the bottom part of the right eye. Draw the outline of the lips with a curve line along the lower left section of the circle.

Draw the outline of the head with a bulge on both upper sides of the head for the ears as shown above.

STEP 5

Draw the outline of the mask with curve lines enclosing the eyes
and both ends tied along the right side of the head.

STEP 6

Draw parallel short vertical line below the head with both ends
connected by a curve line for the base of the body.

Draw the outline of the right arm with parallel diagonal line
from the body going to the right and the outline of the hand at
the end clenched into fist showing four fingers.

Draw the outline of the left arm with parallel curve line from the body curving down towards the left and the base of the closed hand at the end pointing down.

STEP 9

Draw the outline of the weapon shape like a diamond and
appears to be held by the left hand. Draw a tiny circle at the
center of the weapon.

STEP 10

Trace the outline of the body with the collar shape like letter "Y".
Draw the outline of the waist band tied on the front as shown
above.

STEP 11

Draw the outline of the right leg with parallel curve line below

the right bottom part of the body going down and the outline of

the right foot at the end facing front.

Draw the outline of the left leg with parallel diagonal line from the left bottom part of the body going to the left and the outline of the foot at the end facing front.

Final outline. Erase all unnecessary base lines.

STEP 14

You have to color it! White for the head, eyes, hands and feet. Red for the mask and suit. Dark brown for the lower part of the arm and waist band. Light grey for the weapon. That's it! Cute Bear Ninja.

How to Draw Monkey Ninja

STEP 1

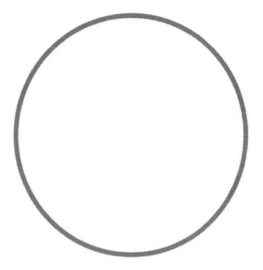

Draw a circle along the upper part of the paper for the base of the head.

STEP 2

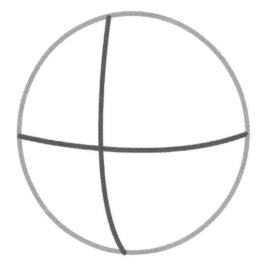

Divide the circle into sections with a curve vertical and horizontal line.

STEP 3

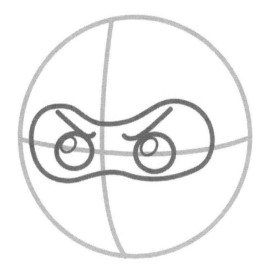

Draw the outline of the eyes with small circles along the horizontal line dividing the head with a small oval inside each for the pupils. Draw a curve line above each eye for the eyebrows. Draw an irregular horizontal oval enclosing both eyes for the opening of the mask.

STEP 4

Trace the outline of the head. Draw succeeding curve line along the top part of the head for the fur. Draw the outline of the eyes with parallel curve lines forming a letter "C" for the left ear and a letter "d' for the right ear.

STEP 5

Draw the base of the body with parallel curve line from the bottom of the head going down with a horizontal oval at the end.

STEP 6

Draw the base of the left arm with parallel slightly curve line from the base of the body going down to the left and the base of the hand at the end. Draw a small circle for the elbow.

STEP 7

Draw the base of the right arm with a curve line from the right side of the body going up to the right ear. Draw the base of the right hand above the right ear holding the katana's handle. Draw the base of the katana's blade between the left arm and the left side of the body pointing diagonally down to the left.

STEP 8

Draw the base of the right leg below the right bottom part of the body. the leg is bended towards the left side with the base of the shoe at the end facing sideward to the left. Draw a small circle for the knee.

STEP 9

Draw the base of the left leg with parallel curve line below the left bottom part of the body going down to the left. Draw the base of the shoe at the end facing sideward to the left. Draw a small circle for the knee.

STEP 10

Draw the outline of the tail with elongated curve line above the right leg.

STEP 11

Trace the outline of the upper suit with the outline of the collar

shape like letter "Y".

Trace the outline of the left sleeve and hand.

Trace the outline of the right sleeve, hand and katana. Draw the

details of the katana.

STEP 14

Draw the outline of the waist band tied along the front. Trace the

outline of the tail.

STEP 15

Trace the outline of the right leg and shoe. Draw the details of the

trouser.

STEP 16

Trace the outline of the left leg and shoe. Draw the details of the trouser.

Final outline. Erase all unnecessary base lines.

You have to color it! Dark blue for the head, ears and suit. White for the inside of the ears and pupils of the eyes. Light brown for the face, hands, chest and tail. Black for the eyes. Grey and light grey for the katana's blade. Grey and dark grey for the katana's handle. Light grey for the collar and upper part of the shoes. Dark grey for the lower part of the sleeves, waist band, lower part of the trousers and shoes. That's it! Monkey Ninja.

About the Author

Kristen Diaz is an accomplished artist and e-book author living in Southern California. She has provided the illustrations for hundreds of children's books as her realistic and lifelike images appeal to children and adults alike.

Diaz began her career as an artist when she was in her 20's creating caricatures on the beaches of sunny California. What started as a way to make extra spending money turned into a successful career because of her amazing talent. Her comically accurate caricatures had a unique look and one of the local authors took notice. When the writer asked Diaz to illustrate one of her books, Kristen jumped at the opportunity to showcase her talent. The result was spectacular and soon Diaz was in high demand. Her ability to change her style to fit the books made her an attractive artist to work with.

She decided to get a more formal education in graphic design and illustration by enrolling in the Arts program at Platt's College which is where she met the love of her life and life partner, Terri. The two live in Pasadena close to the beach where Diaz' career first flourished. She occasionally hangs out on the beach with her easel and paints and makes caricatures of the humanity passing by. Her e-books are simple to follow and contain many witty anecdotes about her life in Pasadena.